A Small Payback, Ode to Victoria Lake

A Small Payback,
Ode to Victoria Lake

Poems
and
Photographs
by
Richard M. Grove

First Edition

Hidden Brook Press
www.HiddenBrookPress.com
writers@HiddenBrookPress.com

Copyright © 2016 Poetry and Photography - Richard M. Grove
Copyright © 2016 Book Layout and Design - HBP

No part of this book may be reproduced except by a reviewer who may quote brief passages in a review. The use of any part of this publication reproduced, transmitted in any form or by any means, electronic, mechanical, photocopied, recorded or otherwise stored in a retrieval system without prior written consent of the publisher is an infringement of the copyright law.

A Small Payback, Ode to Victoria Lake

Poetry and Photography by Richard M. Grove

Layout and Design: Richard M. Grove
Cover Design: Richard M. Grove
Cover Photograph: Richard M. Grove

Library and Archives Canada Cataloguing in Publication

Grove, Richard M. (Richard Marvin), 1953-, author, photographer
    A small payback, an ode to Victoria Lake : poems and photographs / by Richard M. Grove.

ISBN 978-1-927725-31-3 (hardback)

        1. Madawaska (Ont.)--Poetry. 2. Madawaska (Ont.)--Pictorial works.
I. Title.

PS8563.R75S63 2016   C811'.54   C2016-904801-2

On the sign-out board I wrote:
  Gone to heaven in my kayak,
  back soon.

Later I wrote:
  I arrived back but no better heaven
  there than here.

Preface from Richard M. Grove

What a pleasure it has been to visit Camp Madawaska on Victoria Lake for the last few years. Our friend Genevieve (Genny as she is known to us) is the generous hostess of our annual pilgrimage north. Along with other guests we bask in the glory of Northern Ontario. Camp Madawaska is a slice of heaven that holds the sky-filled mirror, Victoria Lake, which in turn holds an ecologically untouched, majestic, tree-covered island known as Weston Island. Victoria Lake is fed by the Opeongo River that flows directly from Algonquin Provincial Park into the loon-skimmed, moose-trudged, lake. Stars sparkle there in the unpolluted black night sky. Wolves yowl their dissonance in the distant echoing hills while bears keep their invisible distance. Thank you, Genny, for the wonderful opportunity provided to us.

Photography has been one of my passions since the age of thirteen with the purchase of my first single-lens-reflect camera that was encouraged and ½ sponsored by my artist, nature-loving father, Marvin Grove. Back in those dinosaur days of film I timidly shot one precious picture at a time. The longest moments would be spent focusing on a subject until I was convinced that I was not about to waste the costly film and processing. The valuable lesson of composition grew out of my restrained student budget.

I love my digital camera. It is an Olympus E-620 with a fabulous lens that zooms from 18 to 180 mm. It is an incredibly versatile lens. I use it for almost 99% of my shooting. My photographer brother, Christopher, put me on to the Olympus. Aside from the relatively low price of the camera, one of the selling features is that it has a stabilizer built into the body of the camera rather than in the lens. It makes for a more affordable collection of lenses. I would like to thank my brother, Christopher, for his tutoring with my camera. He is a marvellously knowledgeable man when it comes to understanding the digital world. He is a large format print technician as well as a fabulous digital designer and photographer. He has taught me much.

On my request for feedback about my working title "An Ode to Victoria Lake", my dear friend John B. Lee made this suggestion about the title – "*I wonder if you might call your book, "A Small Payback" with the subtitle "Ode to Victoria Lake". The idea that this homage to Victoria Lake has its roots in the fact that your father helped you purchase your first camera, and in that you mention the small payback in your dedication. "A Small Payback" might STAND tall and proud like a son returning a gift to a father, a humble offering of gratitude, with the same quality as an offering or a prayer. I see the boy in the man, and in these photos, I see the man who was once a boy, keeping alive what began with the father's gift, the fruits of the seed planted all those years ago when you received your first camera."*

As you see, I took John's suggestion and entitled the book "A Small Payback, Ode to Victoria Lake". For me the title works on a variety of levels. Yes a small payback to my father for his encouragement. The book is also a small payback to Genny, and her parents, Peter and Camilla. The book is also a small payback to Victoria Lake for her pristine beauty.

The first set of images in the book are what I refer to as "digital paintings". They originate as photographs but have been manipulated beyond what I call photographs. They are quite graphic in nature and as an artist require a sophisticated understanding of the Photoshop software that I use. I marque many different layers and treat each seamlessly with its own filter and manipulation. I sometimes say that my digital paintings have as many mouse clicks as a different medium has brush strokes.

The second set of images all have manmade features such as architecture, docks, totem poles, benches, boats, canoes, etc. I quite enjoy shooting and working with different types of subjects. The manmade objects most often have straight, hard geometric lines and curves that are used in the composition of the photograph. An object is not very often just an object. The subjectification of the object is important to me as a photographer. A canoe is not always just a canoe. A picnic table, a roof line, or bright wall are all tools to lead the eye.

The third set of images are of rocks. I love rocks. I love the power they have just by simply sitting there. Their only job is to sit and resist erosion. In a way, all they have to do is be.

The fourth set of images are of plants and fungi. This was somewhat of a problematic section of photographs to include. My joke as a photographer is that I take pictures of anything that does not move, meaning I am not a wild life photographer and generally not a people photographer. That in mind I have to admit that I have done different series of portraits but usually of the person as a stationary subject. The plant life in the Algonquin area abounds. Naturalists of every age run around with identification books for weeds, flowers, fungi, trees and even animal poop. I love nature but I do not profess to be a "Naturalist" with a capital "N". I love shooting flowers, berries, mushrooms etc but I usually see them as colour and form not as species, hence the images of plants are included in this book for artistic reasons. Don't ask me if a type of berry is edible or what kind of flower I have just shot.

The fifth section of images are a short section of only six river photographs. The main river that feeds in and out of Victoria Lake is the Opeongo River, a steady flow of water that is, in the spring, apparently, a raging torrent of bolder-moving, log-pushing muscle of water. I have plenty more river images but sadly I have only ever seen the river in late summer and early fall low-water mode. This has left me with a diminished diversity of river pictures. I have kayaked out of Victoria Lake up river into Algonquin Provincial Park but in low water season one cannot get very far over the surface-dragged boulders that have been smoothed by the millennium. I hope to see the swelled spring runoff one year.

Fog, water and trees; this is the theme of the large last section of photographs. I contemplated creating a section of just fog but those images overlapped with trees and/or water to such a large degree that I put them all together in one large section. This last section of over twenty-five images is my favorite section. Let's call them the landscape pics. I have hundreds of other landscape photographs; I have done my best to pare them down to this number. Because fog is so prevalent in this northern landscape I will start with the moody, sometimes sullen, fog images and finish with the two stunning sunsets to close the book.

All-in-all I am pleased with the poetry, the story, the photographs and the book in general. They are all heartfelt works. I hope you enjoy them as well.

Richard M. Grove / Tai

t

Imagine Here

As for me, my beginner's camera was a Brownie Starmite, acquired at about age fourteen, paid for in full out of my own pocket. The very first photograph I made involved a self-portrait. Standing on my bed, dressed in blue-and-white striped pajamas, holding the camera a few inches from my face, I snapped a close up. The resulting up-nose portrait elongated my proboscis and accentuating a pimple on my chin, proved me in a slightly fish-lensy way to be more of a nerdy Poindexter than sexy young Lothario.

My Mother owned a box camera. She could be counted on to capture decapitations, red heaven, and sweeping landscapes with long shadowed creatures looming on the periphery. "Just shoot what you see," I would say. We would pose, she would insist the sunlight over our shoulder, and click — there we were chin to forehead framed in elm shade, the dog wagging through.

So it seems I came naturally to photographic incompetence. I spent thirty years wasting precious thirty-five millimeter film with a foolproof camera. Now I have a digital. I took it with me to Israel and Jordan. I downloaded the resulting one hundred images onto my computer. From these I could not find a single image worthy of my attention. Meanwhile, I posted one photograph on Facebook. My son wrote me, inquiring, "What is it?"

However, despite my lack of visual acumen I have managed to acquire several friends with a talent for photography. I can recognize a great photograph when I see one. My sister-in-law produced a masterful series of snapshots of architectural beauty of Manhattan. My friend Marty Gervais is world class. He introduced me to Brother Paul Quenon and Bob Hill, both of Kentucky. Bob is a photographer who maintains that all the work is in the darkroom. And then there is Richard M. Grove. He and I recently collaborated on an ekprhastic project on Cuba involving his photographs and my poems. The resulting book, In This We Hear the Light was published in 2013 by Hidden Brook Press. His work is stunning. He has an eye. His visual vocabulary is not limited to landscapes. He captures faces like the best of portrait photographers.

In this book, the one you hold in your hand, you have the spirit of a place. The sky like the geography, is exact and exactly here. Algonquin Park, Lake Victoria, the forest and the water partake of the lovely particulars of the soul of a place, the spirit of a locale. Location. A place of places. Is it the eye that captures the object, or the object that captures the eye? Something of the personality of the viewer inhabits the landscape becoming a revelation, a revealed object of studied attention. Good for you, Richard M. Grove. Tai, my friend, I see what you see. A glimpse of grace. Rare and precious. Essential quiescent. Something we would not have without you.

John B. Lee,
Poet Laureate of the city of Brantford
and of Norfolk County

Windows to Camp Madawaska

I live in Cuba, far from Camp Madawaska, in a different landscape and culture. As a visitor to Canada I have had only a small glimpse of the wonderment that Tai is presenting in this precious book. For me, this book opens two windows to this magical place. One is visual, artistically designed. The photographic images of Camp Madawaska and Victoria Lake bears the imprint of the artist-photographer, the transcendent sense of the man who was there when light was captured in its magnificence. Tai was not alone in that moment he shot each picture. Besides his vast experience as a photographer his visual acuity was also steered by his profound spirituality, which allows him to spot sites in which light, shadows, shapes and colours organize patterns of natural harmony.

The other window to this northern wilderness is opened by a different form of art, closer to the bone, that of the word. Here I find the poet in his full maturity, when soul and mind dwell under summer trees and bear witness of the landscape. There are haikus that match what Tai's pictures have frozen in beauty in a fluid parallelism that provides unified meaning to the overall statement made by the book. There are special moments when nature is humanized by the poet's wish to return to the bliss of simply being, as represented in his poem entitled "I Would Be Happy" where he takes the reader from leaf to grass to bug to rain, and back to earth. As we progress on this walk by the lakeshore, through the woods and over the lake we discover that it is humans who make Camp Madawaska Lodge special as found in his poem entitled, "The People of Madawaska Lodge", this warmth is genuine.

Perhaps the greatest discovery was to find universals, both in pictures and in poems. Here in the Caribbean, on an island with no winter and few running fresh rivers, we also have those brilliant warm grasses; and from his poem "The Dimming Hour" the silence that lasts "till the cricket filled hours of black". So far, so close we are. Thank you, Tai for this magnificent reminder.

Manuel de Jesús Velázquez León
Profesor de la Universidad de Holguín
Holguín, Cuba

Contents

– Preface from Richard M. Grove – *p. vii*

– Foreword from John B. Lee – *p. x*

– Foreword from Manuel de Jesús Velázquez León – *p. xi*

Poems:
- Stoically Standing – *p. 20*
- Poplar Drift – *p. 20*
- Resting In Sun – *p. 20*
- Bringing To Life – *p. 21*
- Cradled – *p. 21*
- She Sings The Stars – *p. 21*
- Red Granit Visitor – *p. 40*
- I Would Be Happy – *p. 41*
- The Dimming Hour – *p. 52*
- Early Morning North of Madawaska – *p. 53*
- My Heart Grows Wings – *p. 64*
- Sky Gliding – *p. 65*
- Kayaking on the Ripples of Indian Summer – *p. 65*
- Intruder Alert – *p. 72*
- The People of Madawaska Lodge – *p. 73*
- Buoyant With Joy – *p. 94*

– A Short Bio – *p. 101*

This book is dedicated to:

my father,
Marvin Grove.
A small payback
for paying for half
of my first serious camera.

Genny
and her parents, Camilla and Peter
for including us in this
fabulous experience.
This book is such a small payback,
a thank you.

my darling wife Kim
for being part
of my life experience.
I could never pay you back
for all the joy.

A Small Payback,
Ode to Victoria Lake

Stoically Standing

Big Dipper slides behind
                silent
white pines

Poplar Drift

a yellow quiver of poplar leaf
                drifts
      on chilled air of September

Resting In Sun

fall's failing flags
                flutter
   resting in sun
on brilliant warmed grass

Bringing To Life

Victoria Lake
        gleefully glistens
                in bright breeze
bringing to life
            Canada's red and white

Cradled

Redding maple leaf
cradled in poplar branches

She Sings The Stars

Wind ruffled Victoria Lake
    sings
her melody of sparkling exaltation.

Red Granit Visitor

Wind-blown foam
curls and swills and ruffles,
pressed against ragged-red
back bone of time.
Lichen clung granite sliding
into amber,
deeper into black,
deeper still to cold
where the serpent of death
presides over sunken logs
laying in sifted silt
for thousands of years.

In this quieted bay
skimmed by loons wardelling
their territorial warning.
I am reminded that
I am a Victoria Lake visitor.

I Would Be Happy

If I could be a leaf
gliding on warm breeze
I would be happy.

If I could be the shinning grass
where leaf would rest
I would be happy

If I could be the bug, the beetle, the ant
that would crawl upon and munch the leaf
I would be happy

If I could be the sparkling, gentle rain
that softens and cools the leaf
I would be happy

If I could be the earth, made of leaf
feeding the tree
I would be happy indeed.

The Dimming Hour

There is a silence in the dimming hour
when the last scraps of day hang
from lemon sliver moon
over stilled amber beach.

There is a silence in the dimming hour
when grey dock shimmers
laughing quietly with silver
tongue's cool lapping.

There is a silence in the dimming hour
when angels sing
in silent silhouettes of haunting pines
clutching shivers of dew filled dusk.

There is a silence in the dimming hour
that will last till the cricket filled hours of black.

Early Morning North of Madawaska
September 14, 2009, 5:30 am

On a silver-sliver-moon morning
I dipped my paddle
into the loon-echoed mist
of Victoria Lake.
Paddling towards waking island,
heavy underbelly of low-slung grey   drags
through black spires,   tree tips pointing
to Venus,   brilliant but fading.

Skimming ebony depths
kayak scrapes to rest
on red sandy shore.
Moments later long-shadow skinny-dip
zings me to life.
Breeze-cradled glide, unpaddled
sails me back as golden morning rises,
       others now stirring.

My Heart Grows Wings

Ebony branches part
to brilliant sundrenched view
down, down over tree tip spires
to vast wilderness panorama
unsullied, pristine.
Wing tips dip,
loon lances
silver mirrored sky

*Note: The title for this poem came from a line in the poem
"Autumn Burial" by Glen Sorestad*

Sky Gliding

Grey roots clutch
yellow sand bank
ready to slide
any moment
a century from now
over granite bolder strewn shore
into silent
breeze rippled Victoria Lake.

Loons dip and dive
to chilled dark depths
corking to surface
wardling a warning
shy of sky gliding
kayak approach.

Kayaking on the Ripples of Indian Summer

leaves chatter against gentle giggling shoreline-lappings
sun warms bare legs after cold paddle-dripping sparks zing
breeze carries me like a lullaby
    east
        home
            resting
after restorative invigorating strokes into fall=s black bay
yin and yang balance restored
                soul sings

Intruder Alert

Our human footprints pressed
soft, into yellow sand, side by side
with wolf, bear, deer, moose.
We are trespassers on their beach
hopping from the luxury
of motorized pontoon boat,
tea biscuit in hand,
kicking off sandals with glee, tourists
in the wilderness of wonder. Loons wardle
in safe proximity telling us to stay away –
intruder alert, intruder alert. As visitors
we tread carefully with marvel leaving
nothing but our footprints.

The People of Madawaska Lodge

The people, are friendly and warm,
as gentle as the breeze that tickles
the silver lapping shimmers of Victoria Lake
swaying the time drifted pines patiently standing.
The friends of Madawaska Lodge cling
gently to now, never letting go of peace as it floats
from bobbing dock, to raft, to sanded shore, under sliding sky.

The people are what lure me to the granite lined shores
to bask in worry free kayak, freckled by glistened paddle spray.
The people are what draw me
to the one hundred-year-old log cabin, her red and white trim,
grey ample deck of languid snoozes.
As grand as the landscape, as grand as the sky, the water
it is the people, the varied people
that make Madawaska Lodge special.

Buoyant With Joy

We eleven, buoyant with joy, gay with the abandoned pleasure of children as if dragged on a hay wagon with the important mission of nil, cackling and smiling and chortling under grey but promising skies, clenching collars closed, some hatted or hooded against brisk wind from the west. Our canopied, Madawaska pontoon boat chugging along, gurgling its serpent's breath with the mission of mooring at the head of Sea Lake Trail, bright ribboned for Victoria Lake-side approach.

Bare-footed, calf deep, boat was guided and carefully lashed to shore, anchor hung in tree. We nimbly rock-hopped to shore to start our up-hill trek in search of brush-hidden canoes. After valiant bolder clambering we dwindle to nine as moss-covered ankle turners threatened our harmonious trudging.

With continued childlike, gay abandon we tip canoes into lapping welcome of Sea Lake and ponder the delicately chosen seating arrangements for nine in two gently buffeted canoes. A man of ample girth is directed to the middle floor of canoe number one. Ballast securely stowed three others are maneuvered into push-off position. Two of us face north and two of us face south, the oddest canoe paddling configuration ever imagined. Ballast man in middle is entrusted with one of the three paddles.

Canoe number two is gingerly arranged with the remaining five; a metal cookie tin stacked with fragile shortbreads, shoulder to shoulder, fitting one last cookie for good measure so Aunt Mary will have the pleasure of another delicate delight.

Heave hoe and off we go, for a merry old jaunt indeed. Gay abandon quickly turns to gunnel tipping caution. With a joyful sense of trepidation ballast man's backwards facing partner asks, "what is the purpose of this exercise?" to which there is no possible sane reply.

Silver-tonged, gunnel-lapping steers us for a quick sightseeing tour of the petite shining gem bordered by emerald, stoically standing pines. A wide berth is given to any possible side swiping calamity. Timidity and slow leak in canoe number two cuts our jaunt to a wisdom-guided termination.

Landing and disembarkation was tip-toe flawlessly executed. With canoes tipped back to shore we trundled with glowing hearts back to pontoon boat where Mr. and Mrs. Ten and Eleven greeted us in relaxed, cheerful equanimity. Celebrations of our flawless excursion ensued.

A Short Bio:

Richard M. Grove was born into an artist family in Hamilton, Ontario, on October 7, 1953. With both parents artists and gallery owners, he had a unique and early introduction into the world of visual art. His first experience with art was with photography when at the age of thirteen he purchased, with his father's enthusiasm and help, his first single lens reflex camera. Over the ensuing years, after leaving high school, he studied pottery at Mohawk College, design and pottery at Sheridan College, leading to his graduating in 1984 from the Experimental Arts Department at Ontario College of Art. In 1994 he graduated with honours from the Humber College, Arts Administration diploma program. In 2002 he returned to school to study computer courses relating to publishing. Since graduating from OCA, Richard has exhibited in more than twenty, solo and group exhibitions in Hamilton, Toronto, Boston, Calgary and Grand Prairie. He has his art in over thirty corporate collections across Canada, the most prominent of which are Esso Resources, Continental Insurance, Alberta Energy Corporation and Calgary District Hospital Group. These four companies alone represent a collection of almost thirty pieces of his work. Among the many corporate collections are six commissions of different styles and mediums ranging from pastel on paper to acrylic on canvas.

Along with his visual art, Richard, otherwise known to friends as Tai, has been writing poetry seriously for decades and has had over 100 of his poems published in periodicals and has been published in over 30 anthologies from around the world. He is an editor and publisher and runs a growing publishing company, Hidden Brook Press, from which he publishes books of every genre for authors around the world. Aside from being a published poet, Richard has also exhibited his poetry in acrylic on paper paintings as well as in audio sculptures.

Richard is the founder of the Canadian Poet Registry, an archival information website that lists Canadian poets including: biographical information, their book titles and awards. One can view this website at - http://www.hidden brookpress.com/Registry.htm. He was an active member of the Canadian Poetry Association (CPA) for ten years serving on the executive for seven years including five as President. He is the founding president of the CCLA– Canada Cuba Literary Alliance (2004) – www.CanadaCubaLiteraryAlliance.org. He is also the founding president of the Brighton Arts Council. Richard has also been a public speaker, MCing poetry readings and other literary events. He has been invited by a number of literary groups as Feature Speaker on various topics in Cuba, Germany, USA, New Zealand and Canada. He was also the Feature Author as publisher/poet in the October 1998 issue of "The Treasure Chest" published out of Virginia, USA and Feature Poet in "Poetry Canada" in 2004. Richard now lives with his wife, Kim, also a writer and editor, in Presqu'ile Provincial Park situated halfway between Toronto and Kingston, south of the 401 hwy. Their location is a constant inspiration for their work.

Other books by Richard M. Grove

This book and others are available on Amazon.ca and .com

Photography and Digital Painting:

Sky Over Presqu'ile
Digital Paintings and Poems by Richard M. Grove
ISBN 1–894553–51–9

terra firma
Photography by Richard M. Grove
ISBN 978-1-894553-82-7

Oxido Rojo
Photography by Richard M. Grove
ISBN 978-1-894553-75-9

Substantiality
Digital Paintings by Richard M. Grove
ISBN 978-1-894553-74-2

North of Belleville
Poetry by James Deahl
Photography by Richard M. Grove
ISBN – 978-1-897475-19-5

In This We Hear The Light
Poetry by John B. Lee
Photography by Richard M. Grove
ISBN – 978-1-897475-96-6

Beyond the Seventh Morning
A poetry anthology with
b/w Photography by Richard M. Grove
ISBN – 978-1-897475-95-9

Poetry, Short Stories and Memoir:

Beyond Fear and Anger
ISBN – 0-9699598-0-X

Poems For Jack: Poems for the Poetically Challenged
ISBN   0 9699598 0 X

A View of Contrasts: Cuba Poems
ISBN 1-894553-02-0

Cuba Trip – e-Book
ISBN 1-894553-72-1

The Family Reunion
ISBN 978-1-894553-90-2

From Cross Hill
ISBN 978-1-897475-15-7

Psycho Babble and the Consternations of Life
ISBN 978 0 9732522 2 4

a trip to banes, Cuba, 2002
ISBN 978-1-897475-02-7

Trapped In Paradise – Views of My Cuba
ISBN 978-1-897475-57-7

The Importance of Good Roots
ISBN – 978-1-897475-97-3

Destination Cuba: A Cuba Memoir
ISBN – 978-1-927725-10-8

Living in the Shadow
ISBN – 978-1-927725-35-1

www.ingramcontent.com/pod-product-compliance
Lightning Source LLC
Chambersburg PA
CBHW041508220426
43661CB00017B/1284